A Coloring Book for Girls

BEAUTY
COLORING BOOK

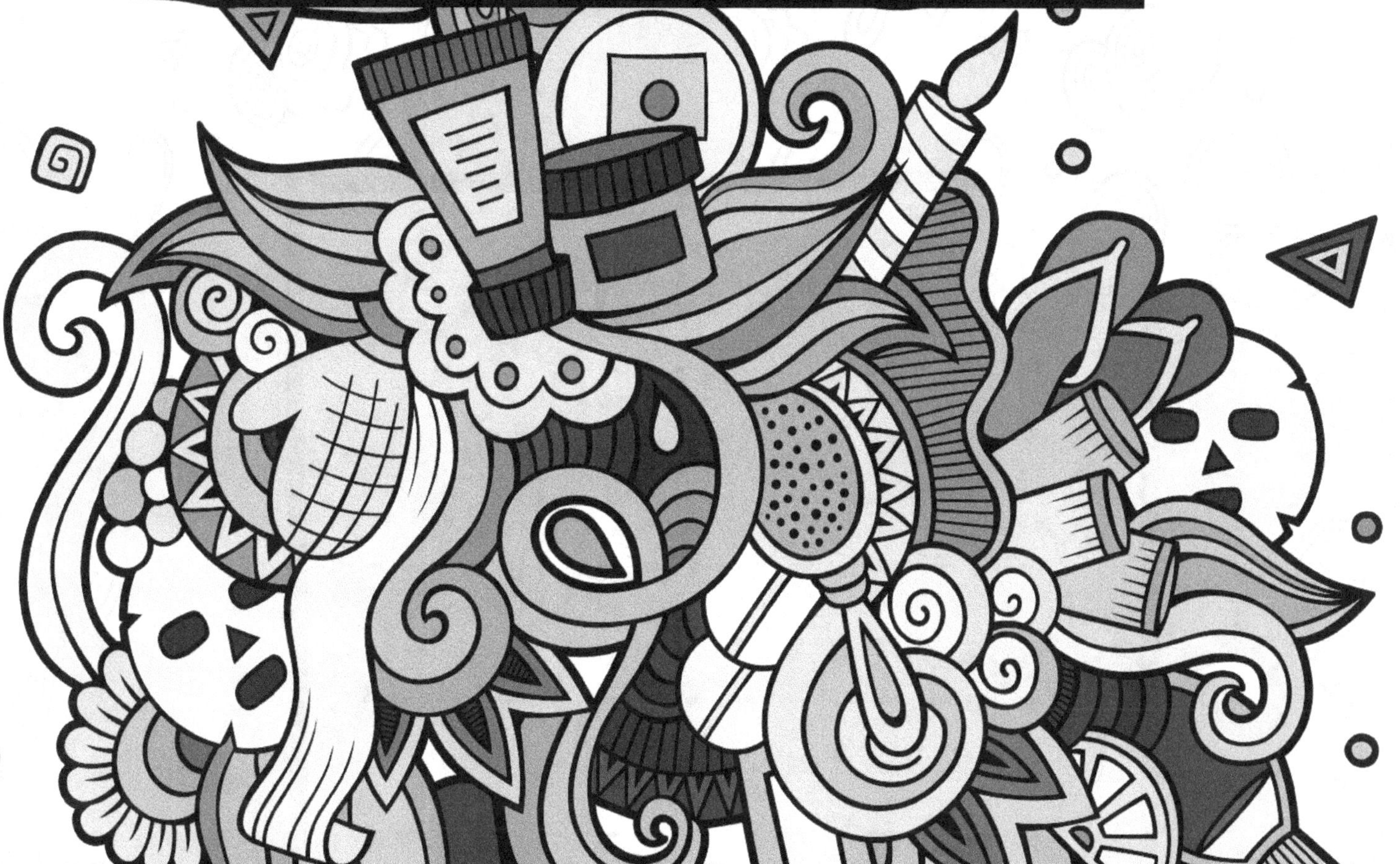

COLORING BOOKS
FOR ADULTS

This Book
belongs to

TEST YOUR COLOR

FAV

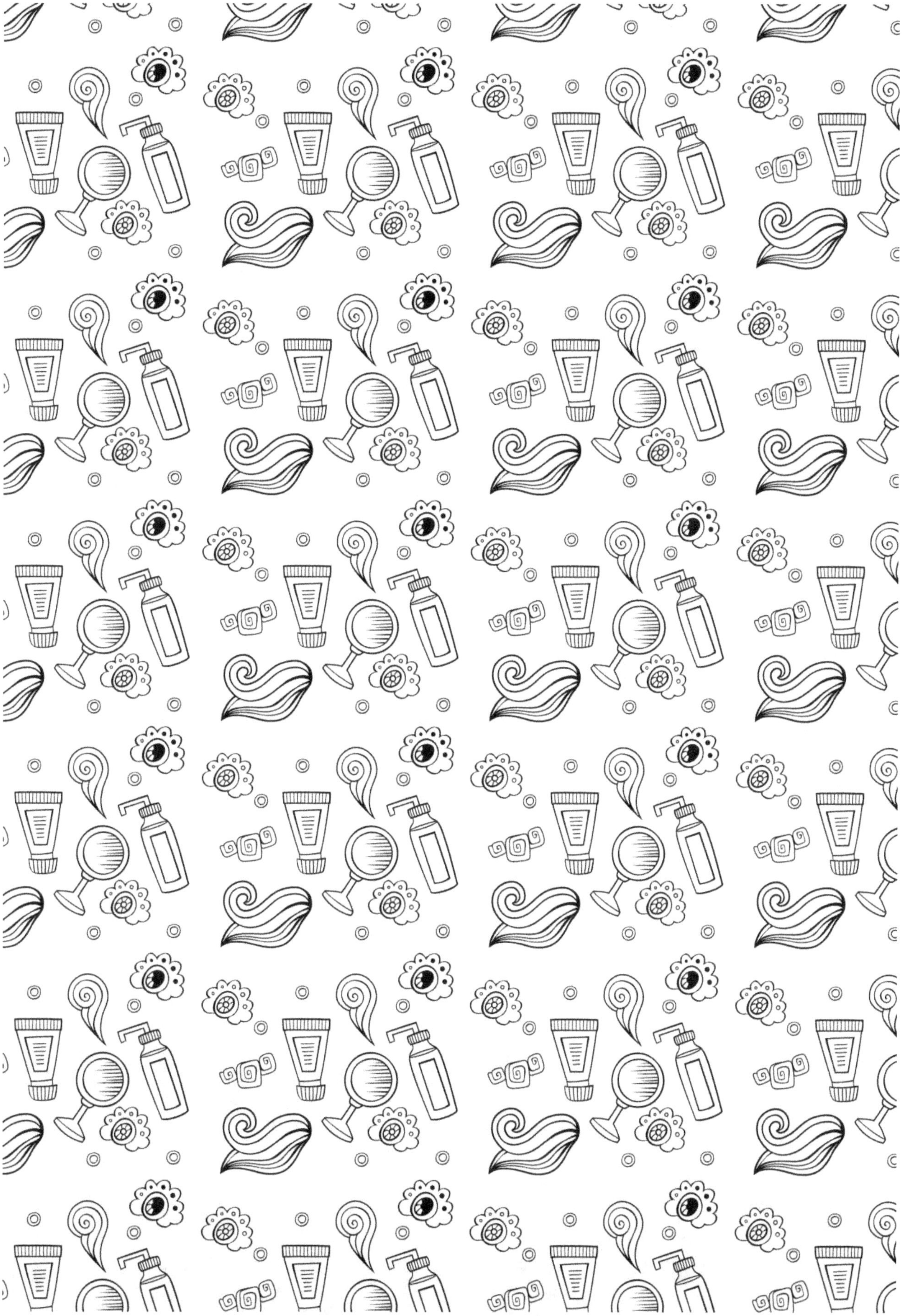

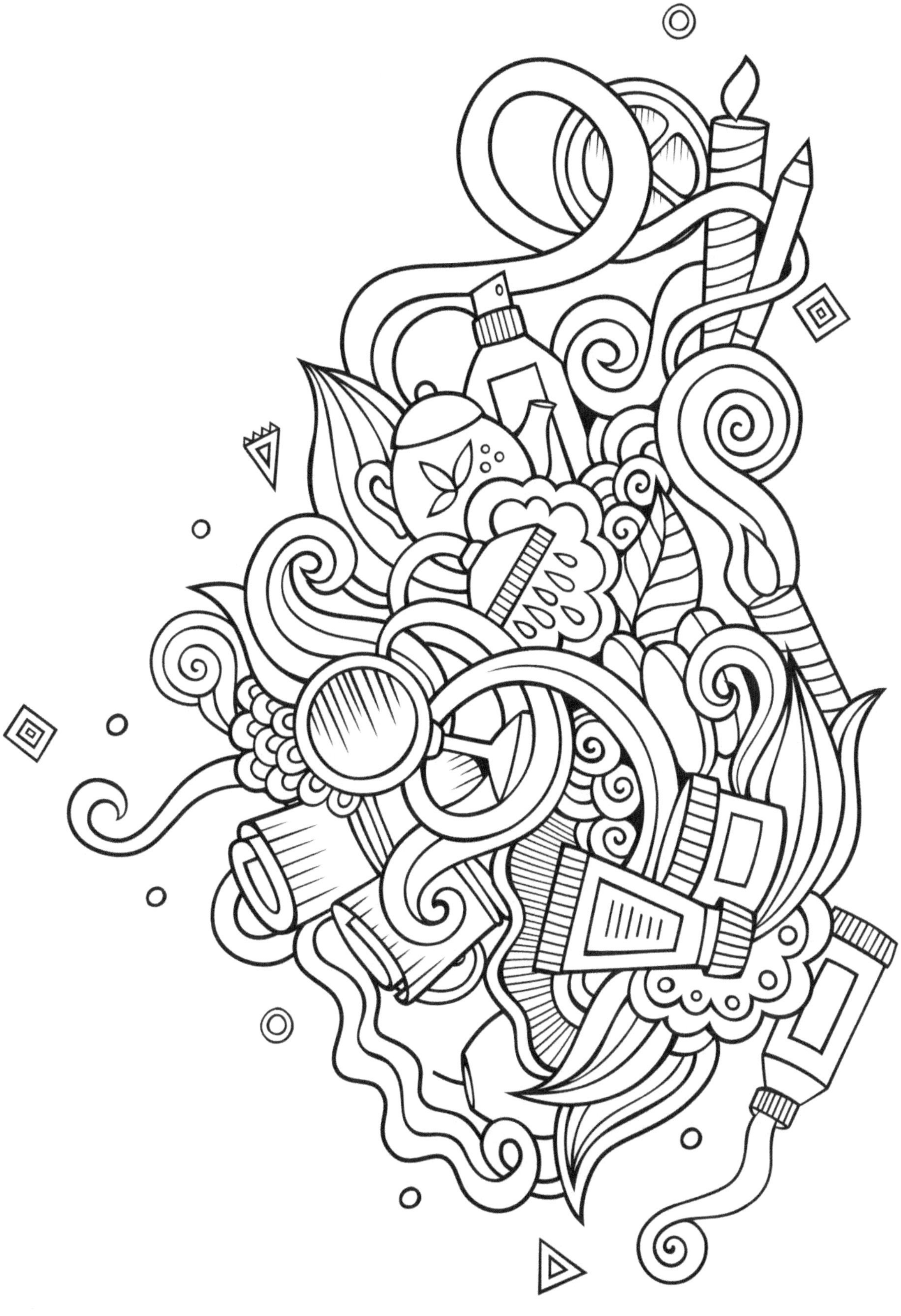

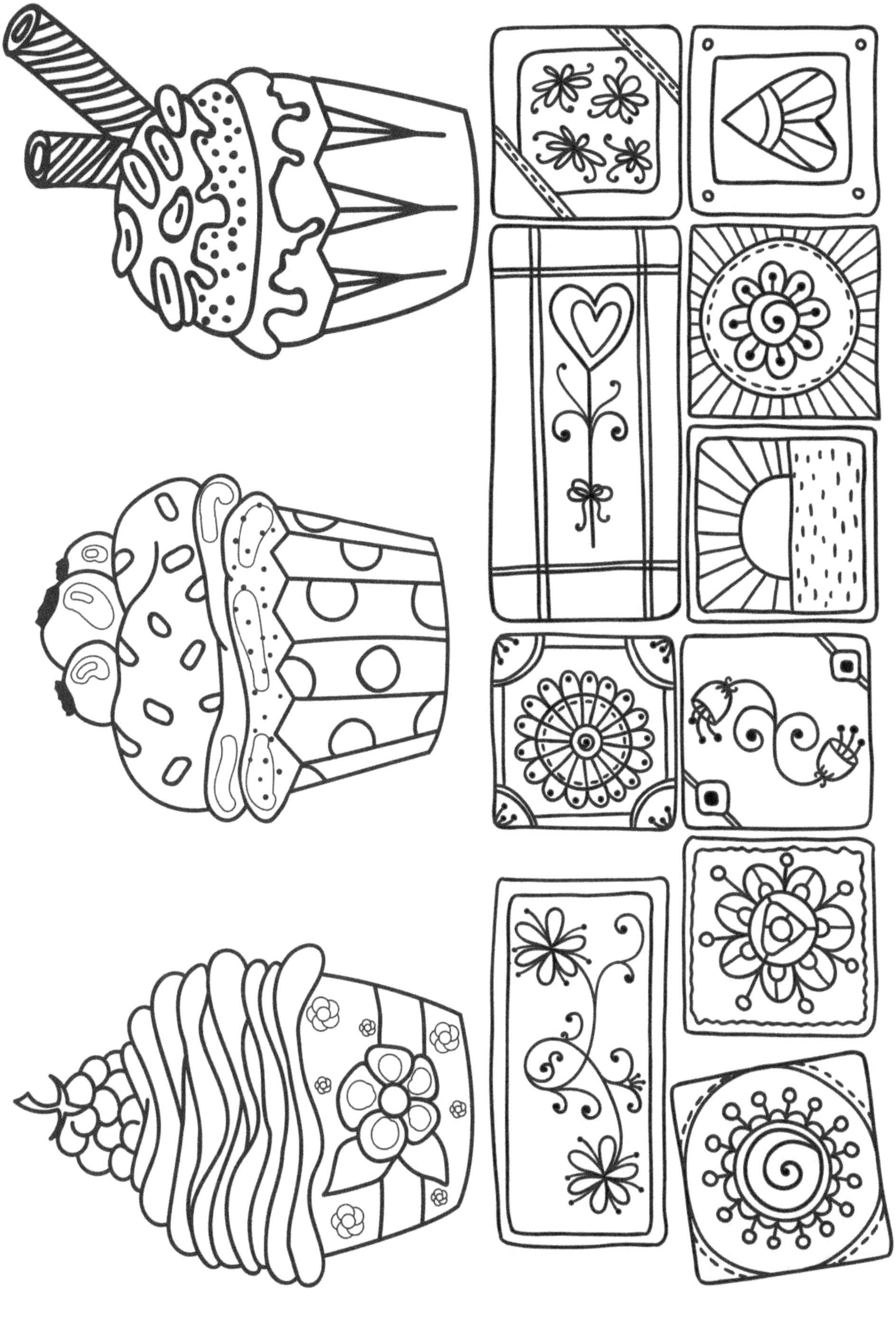

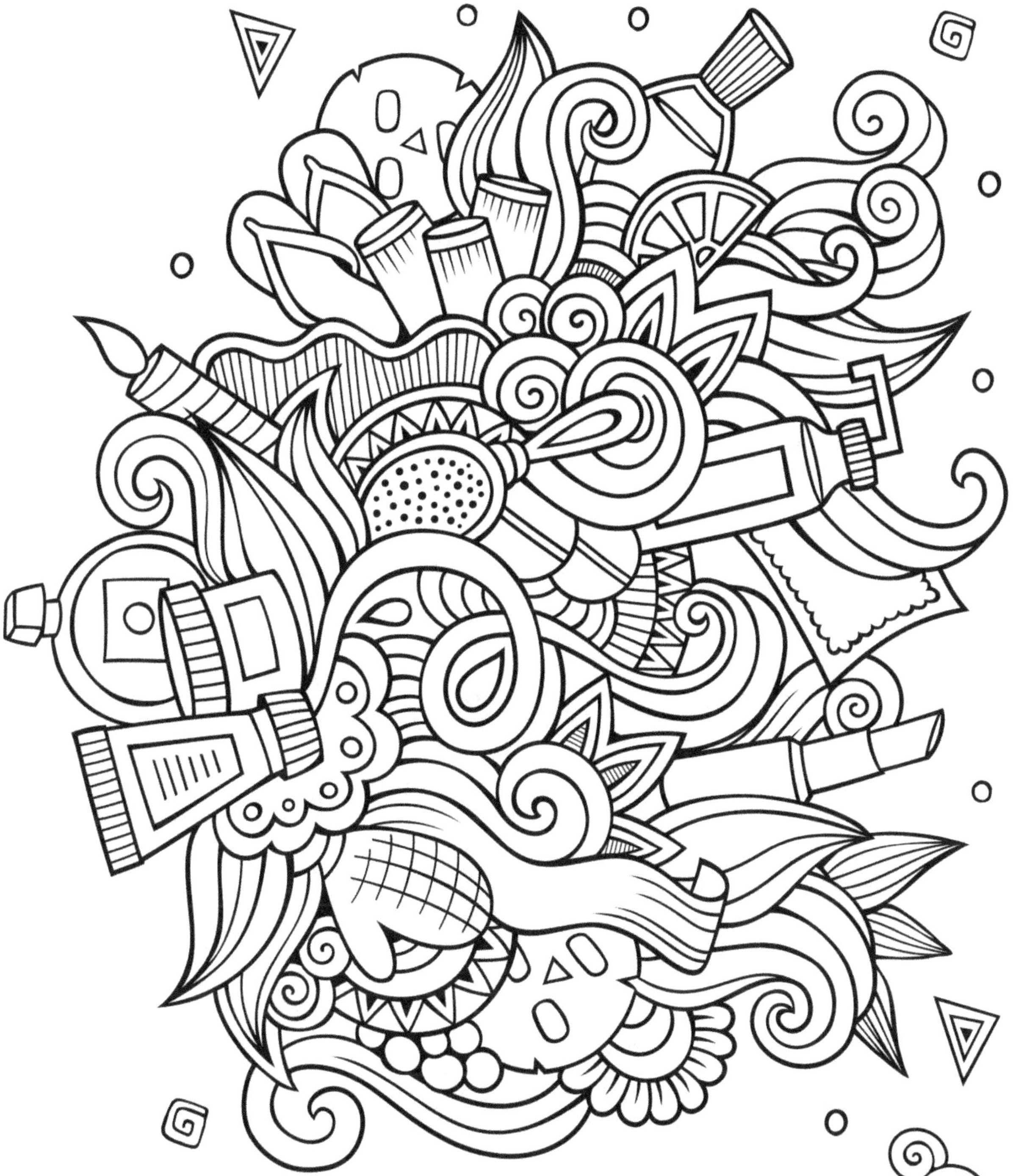

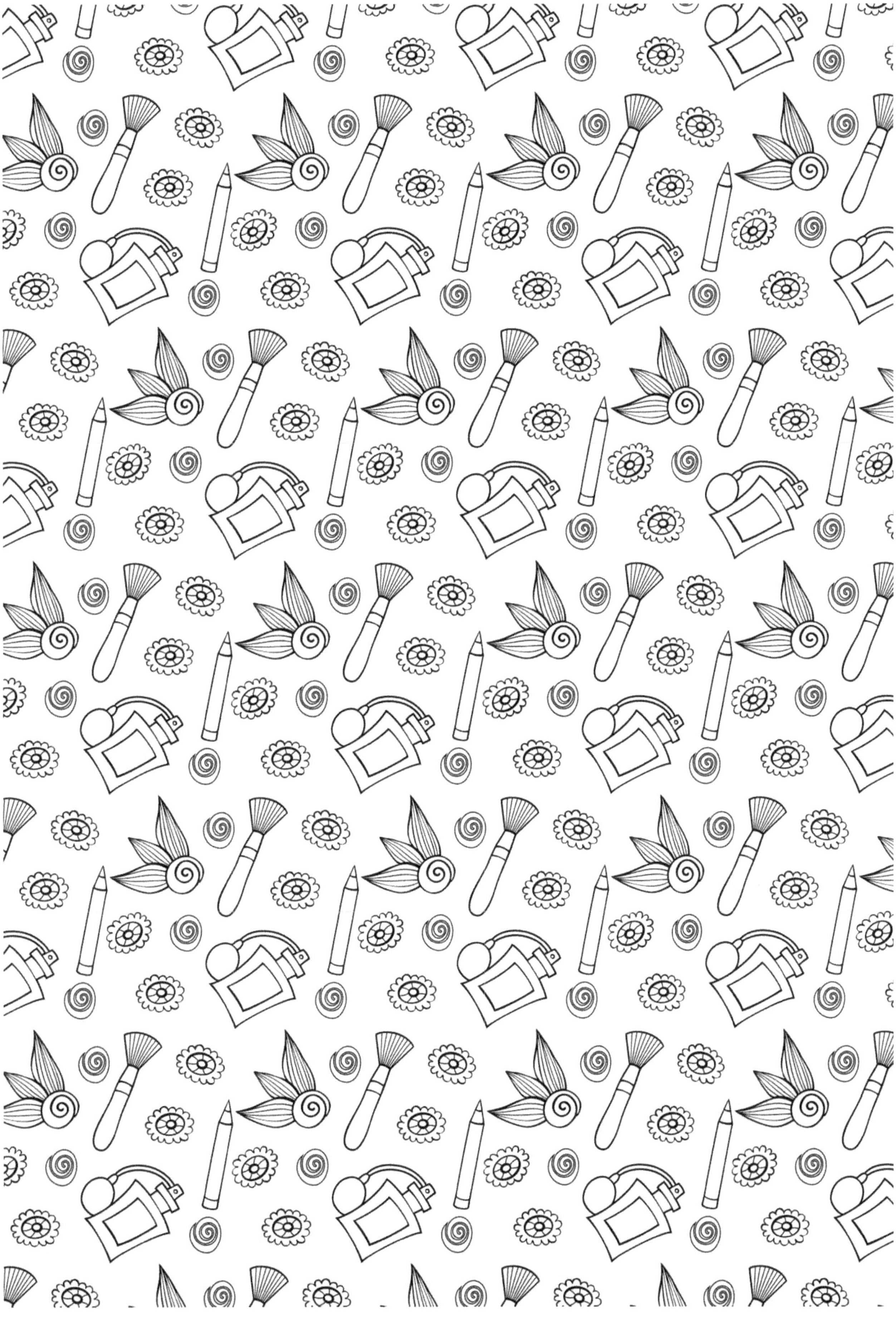

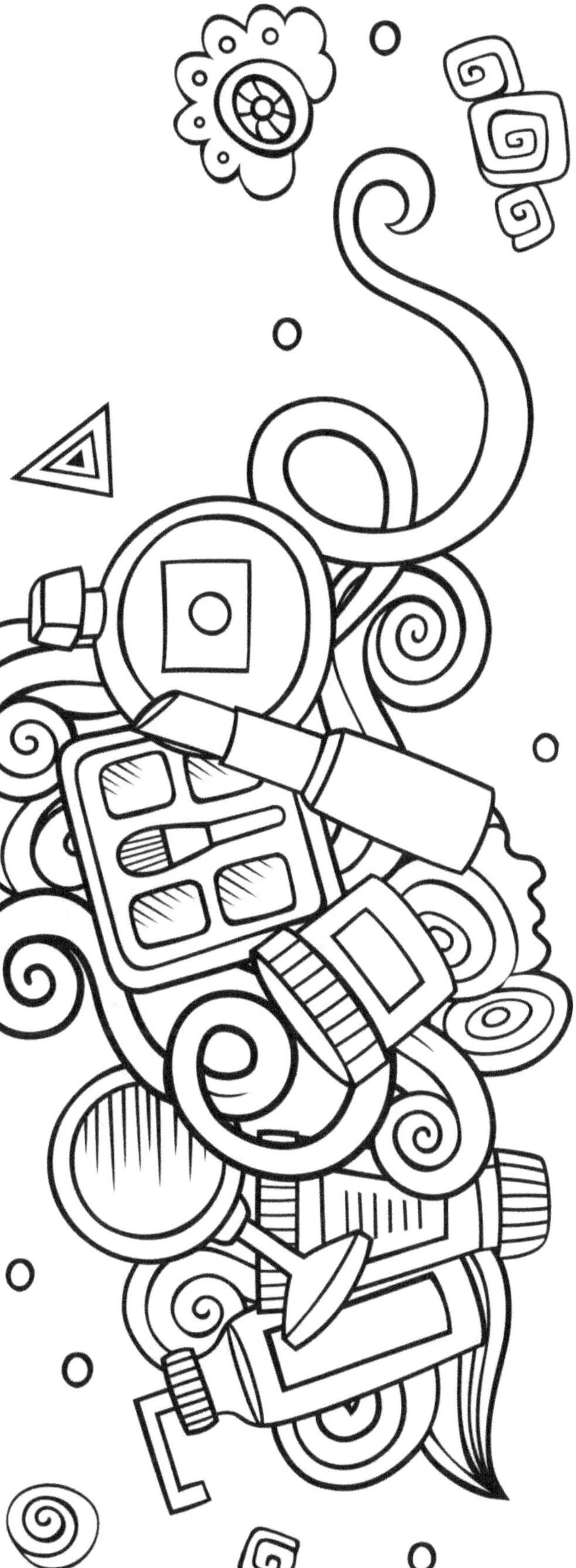

I ♥ U!

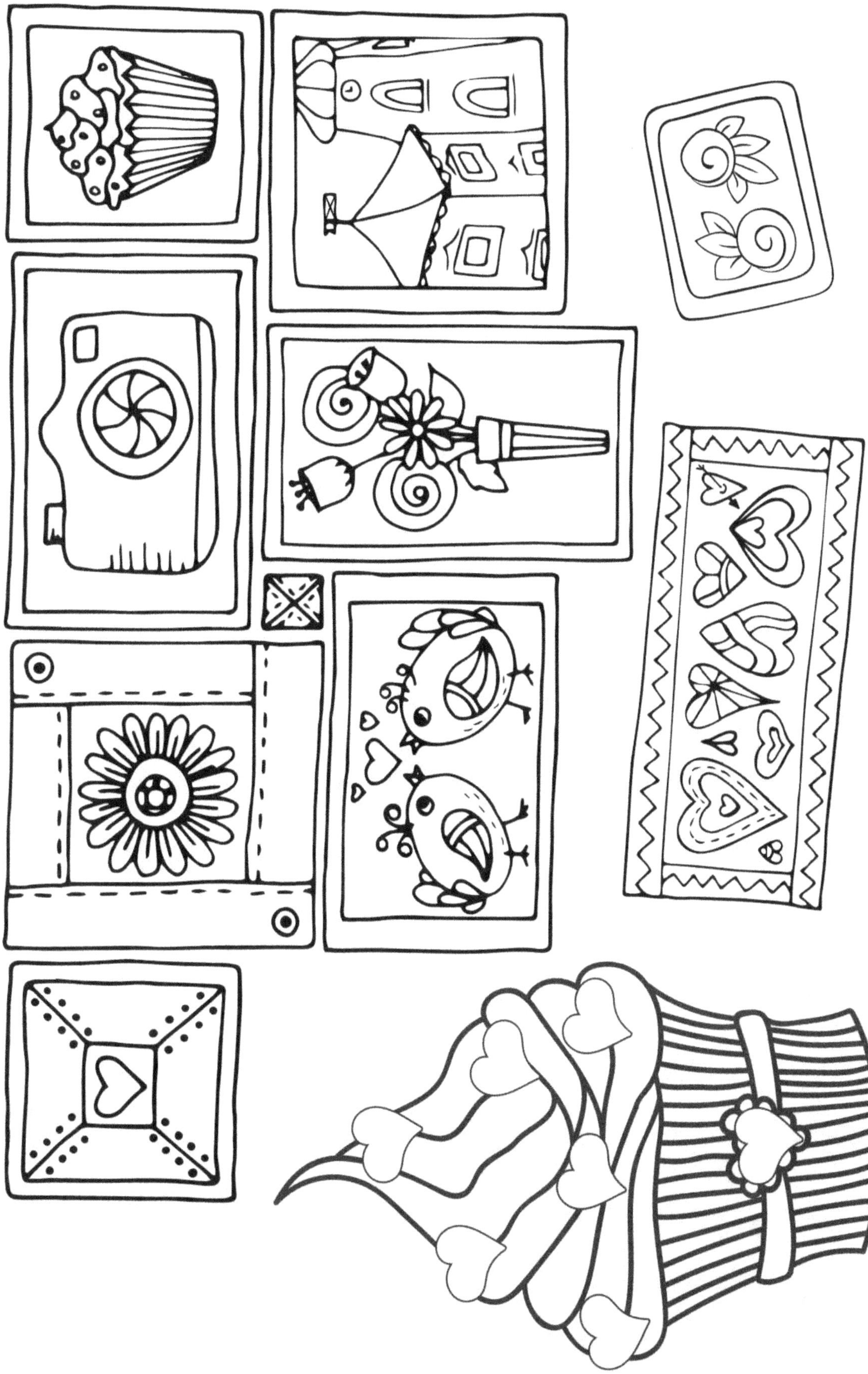

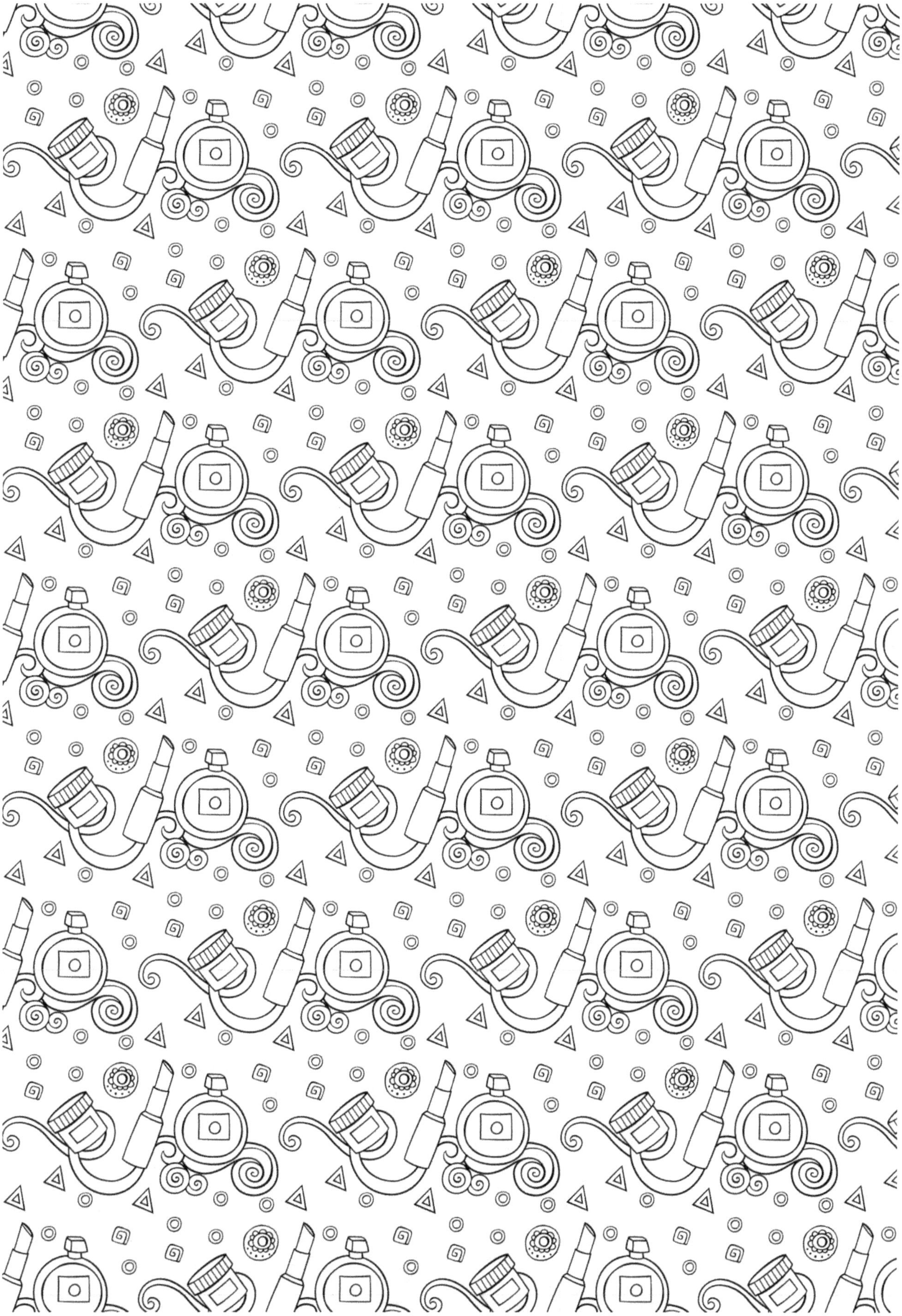

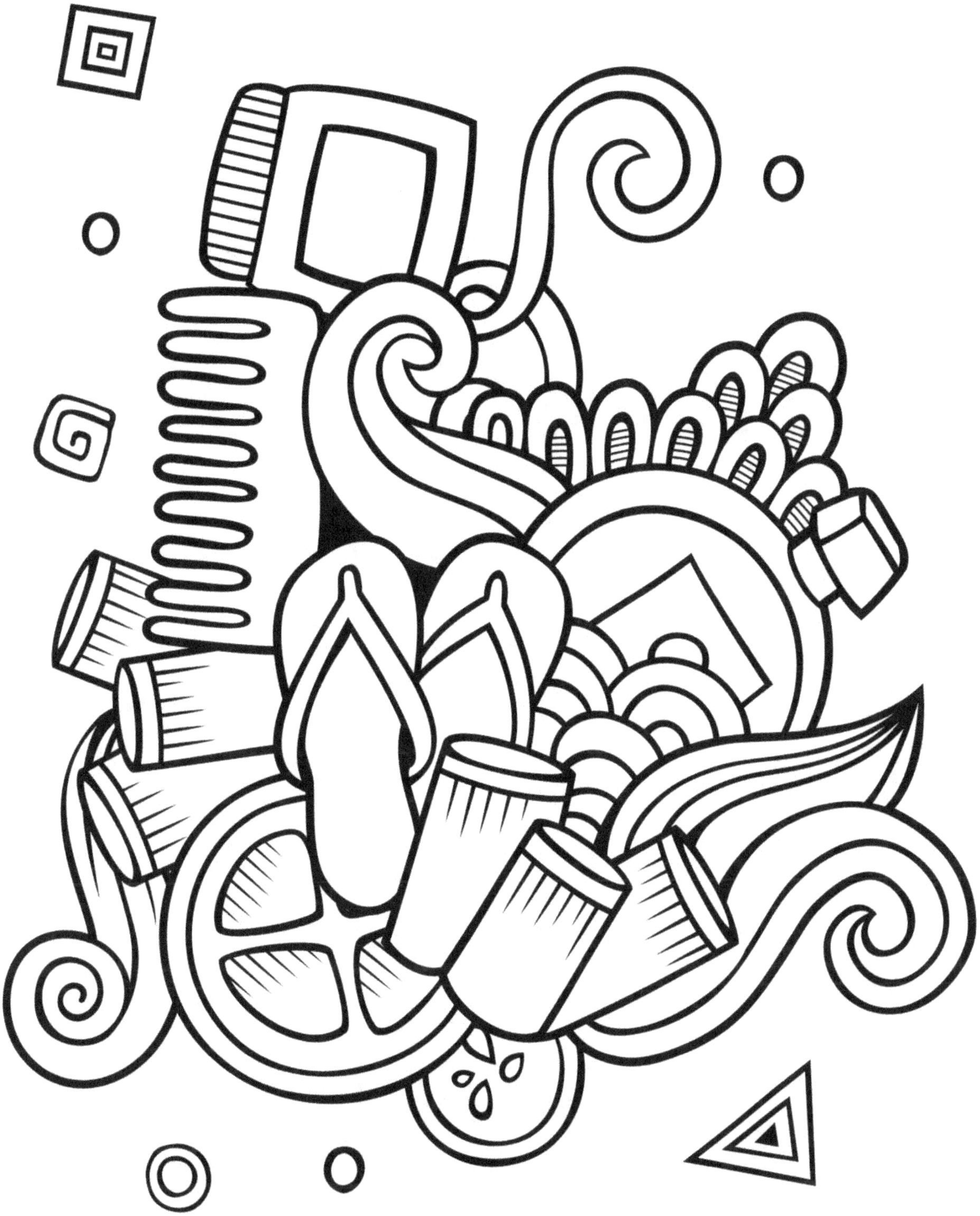

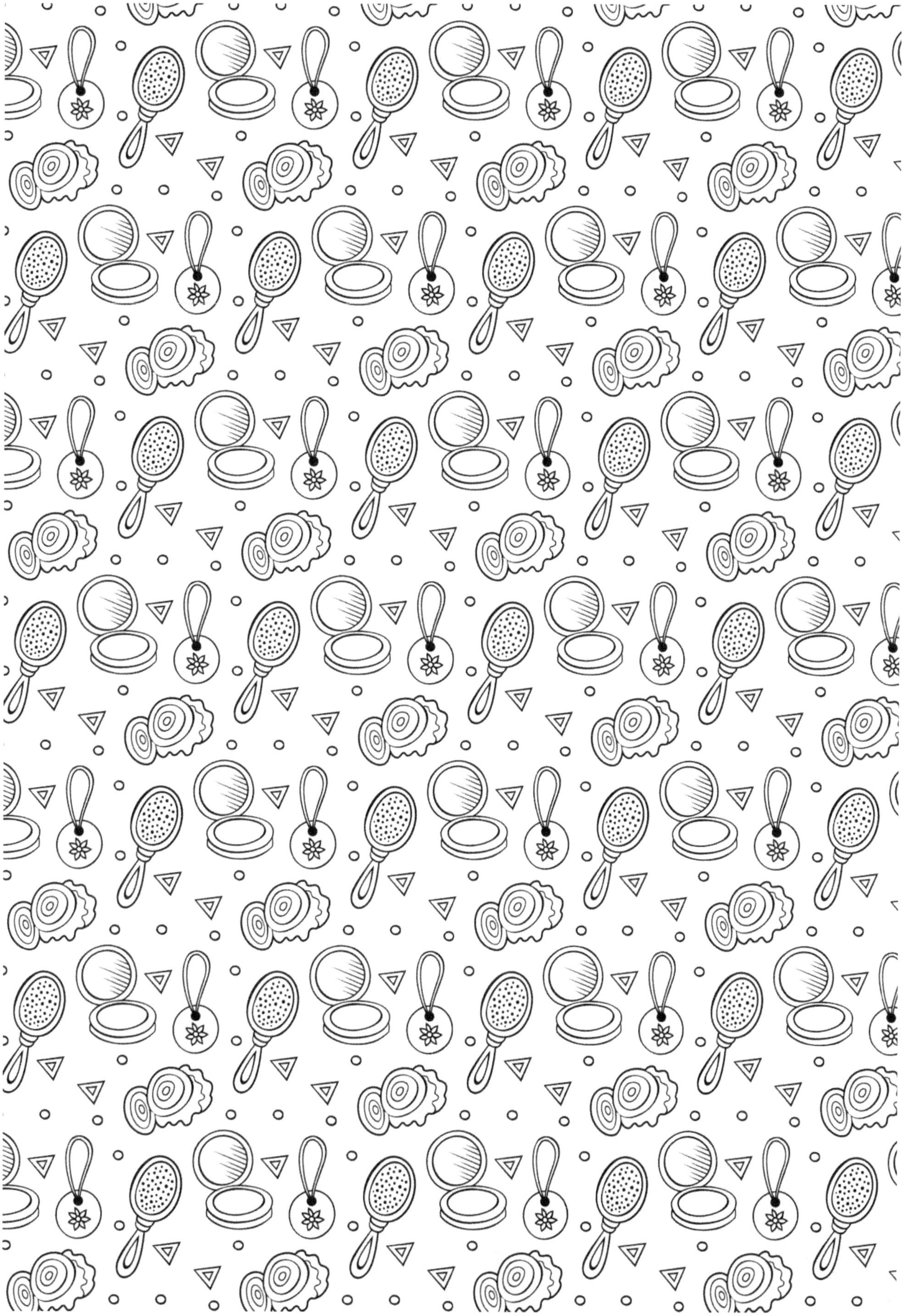

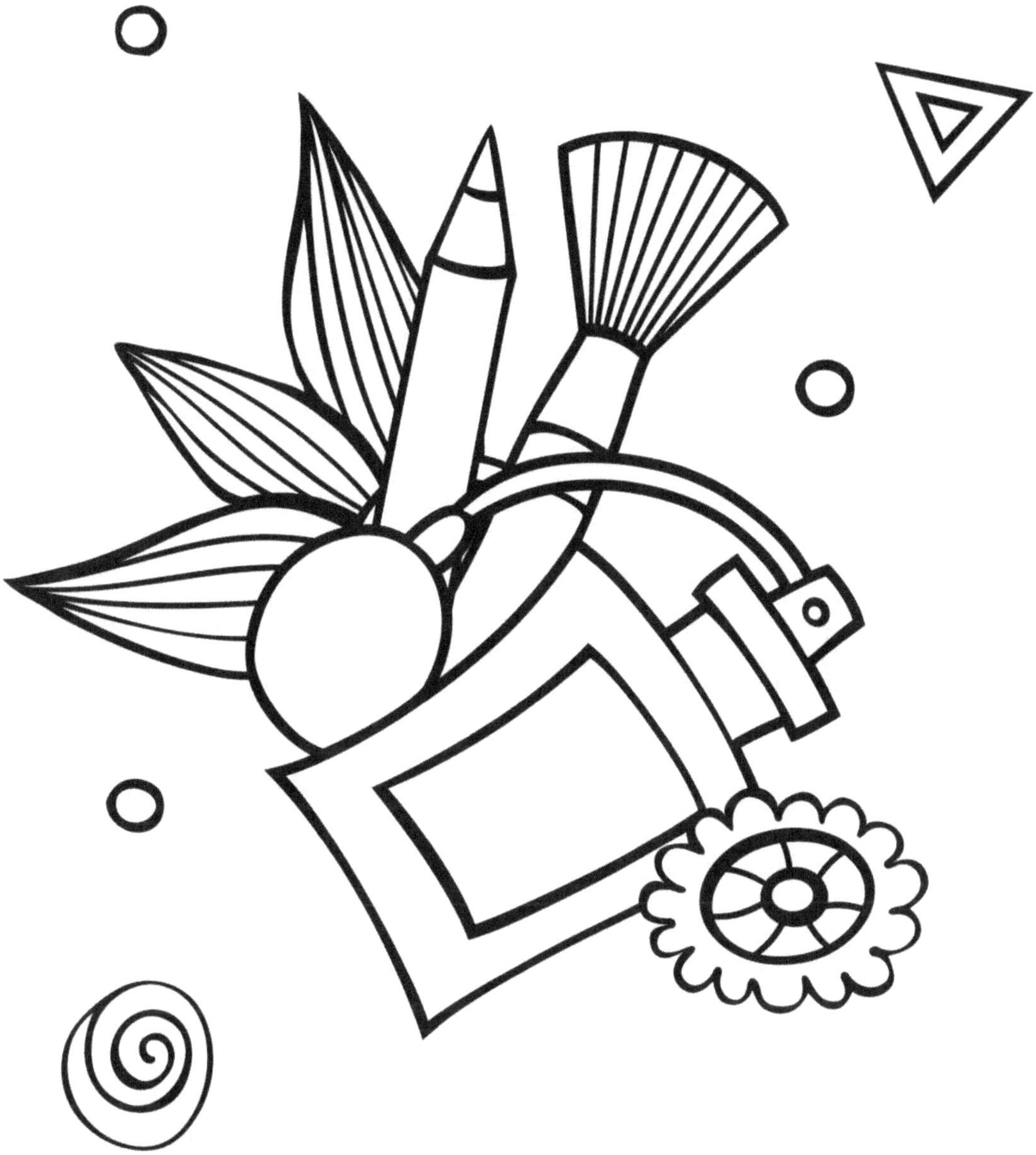

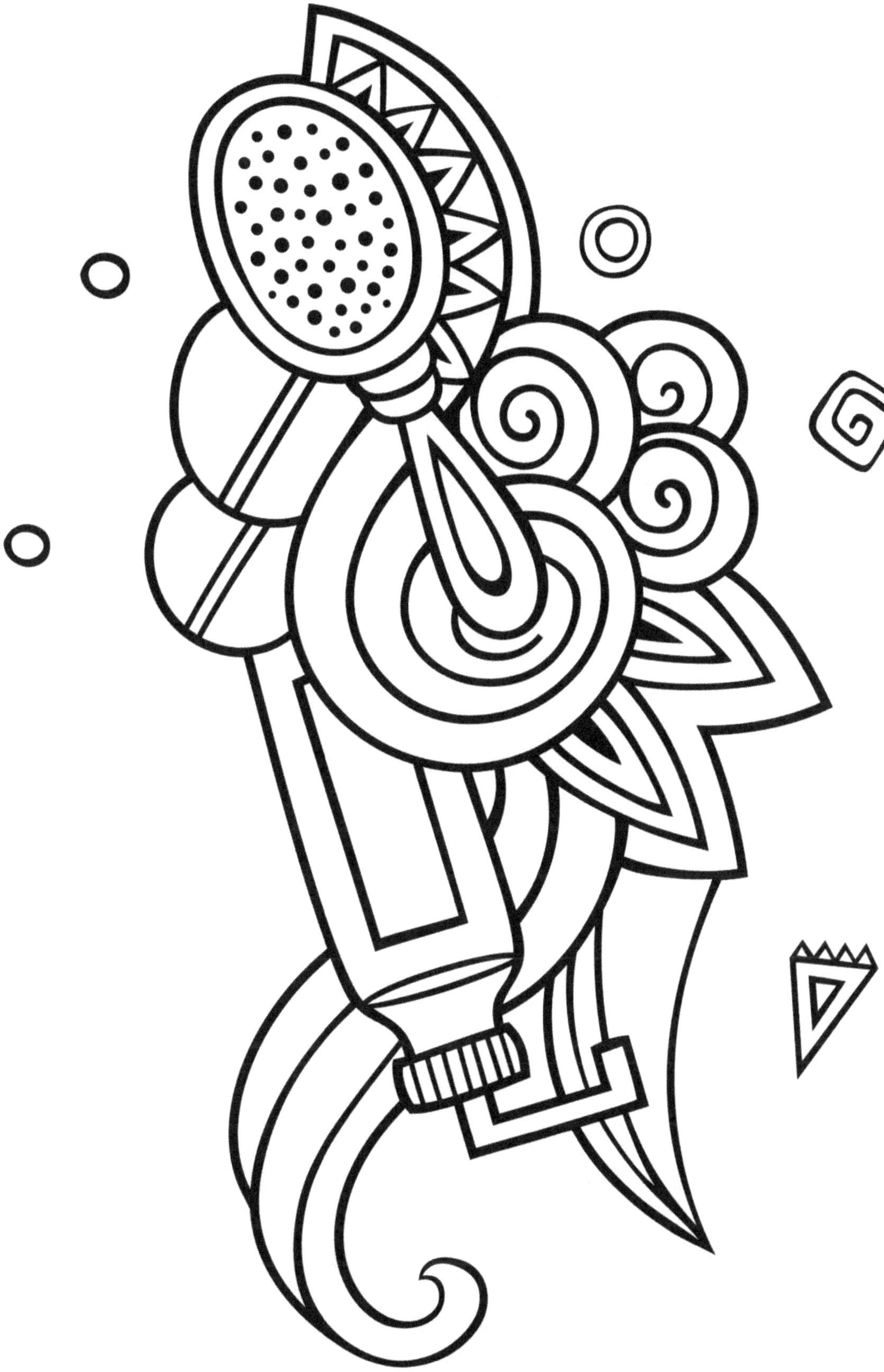

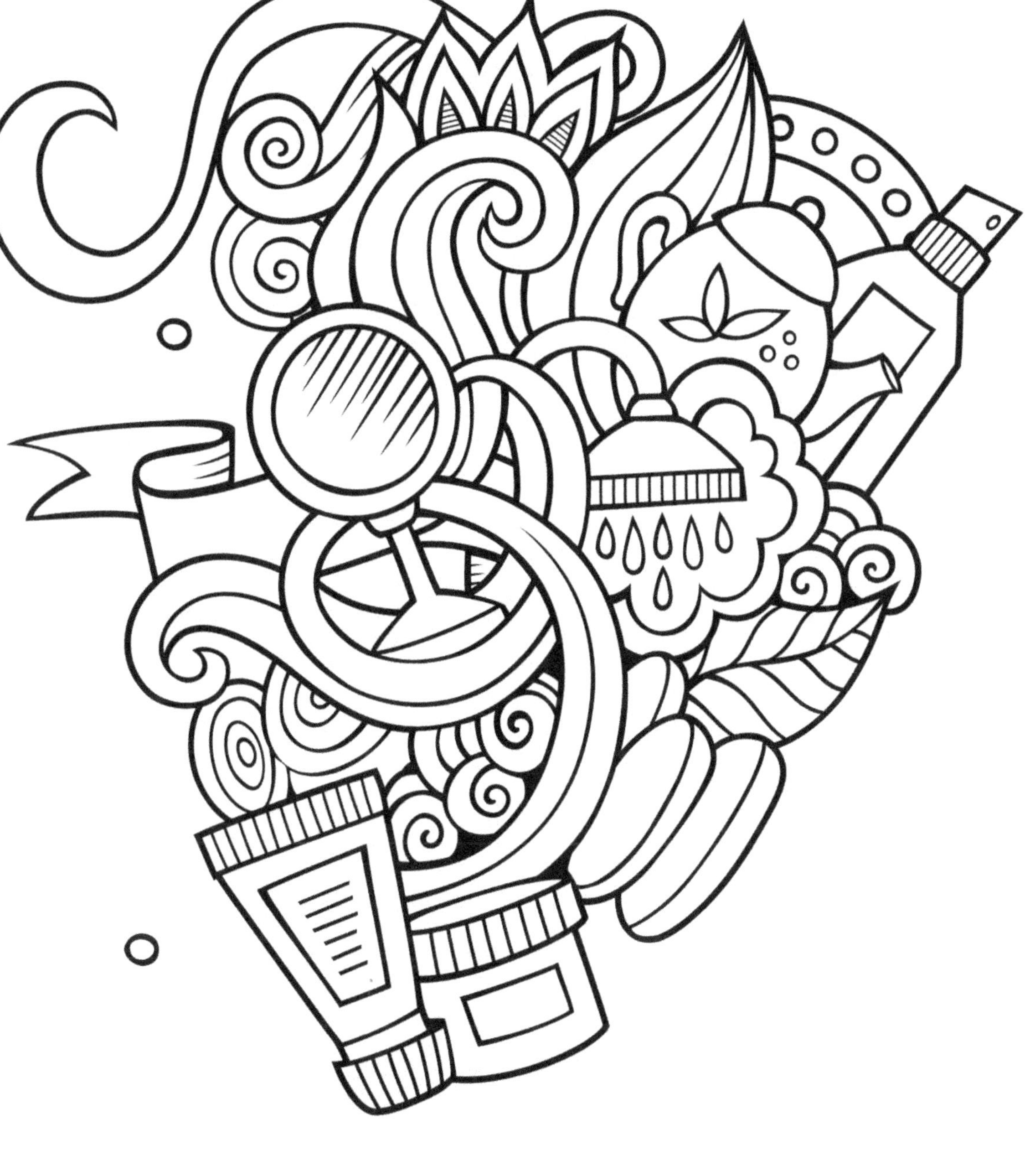

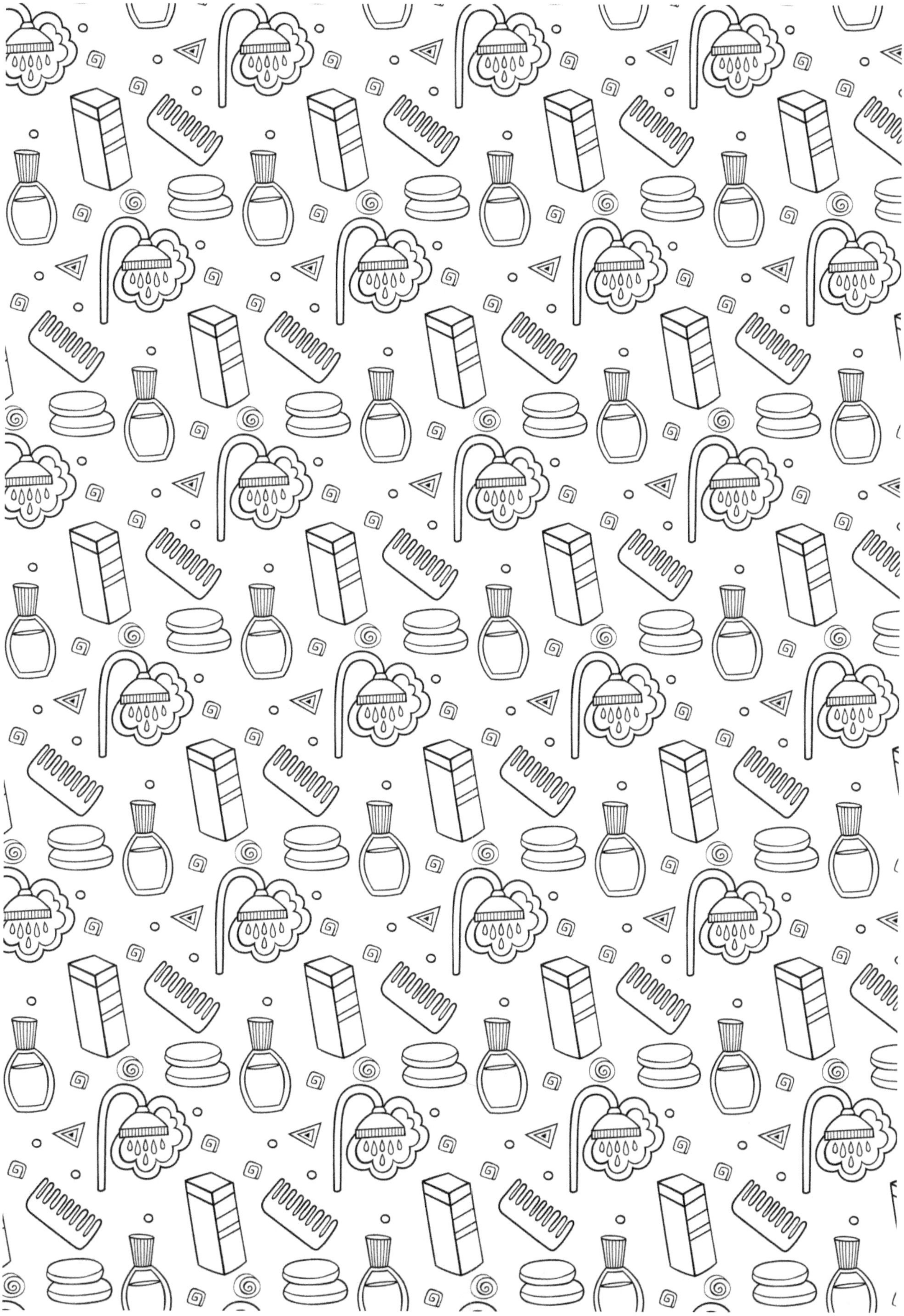

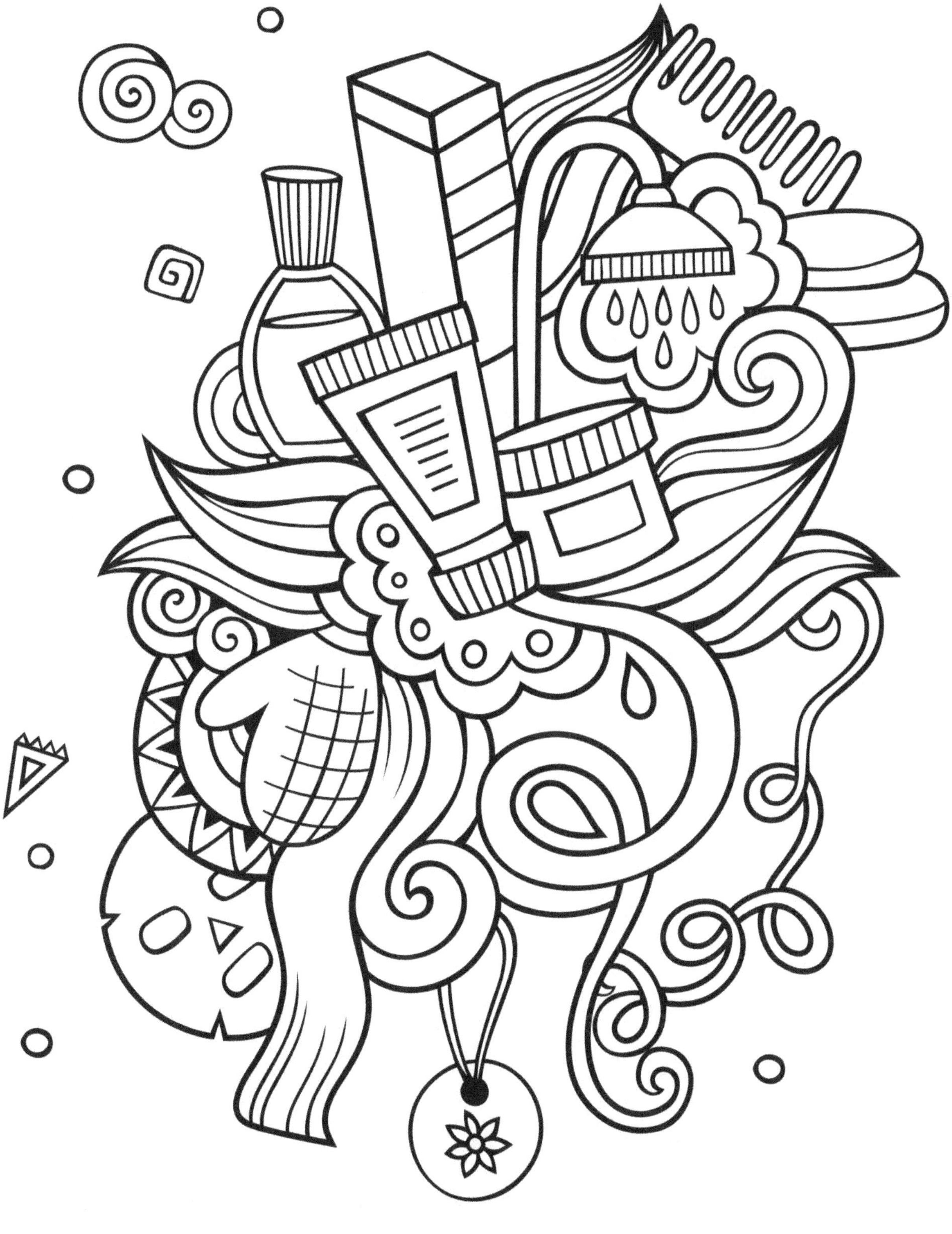

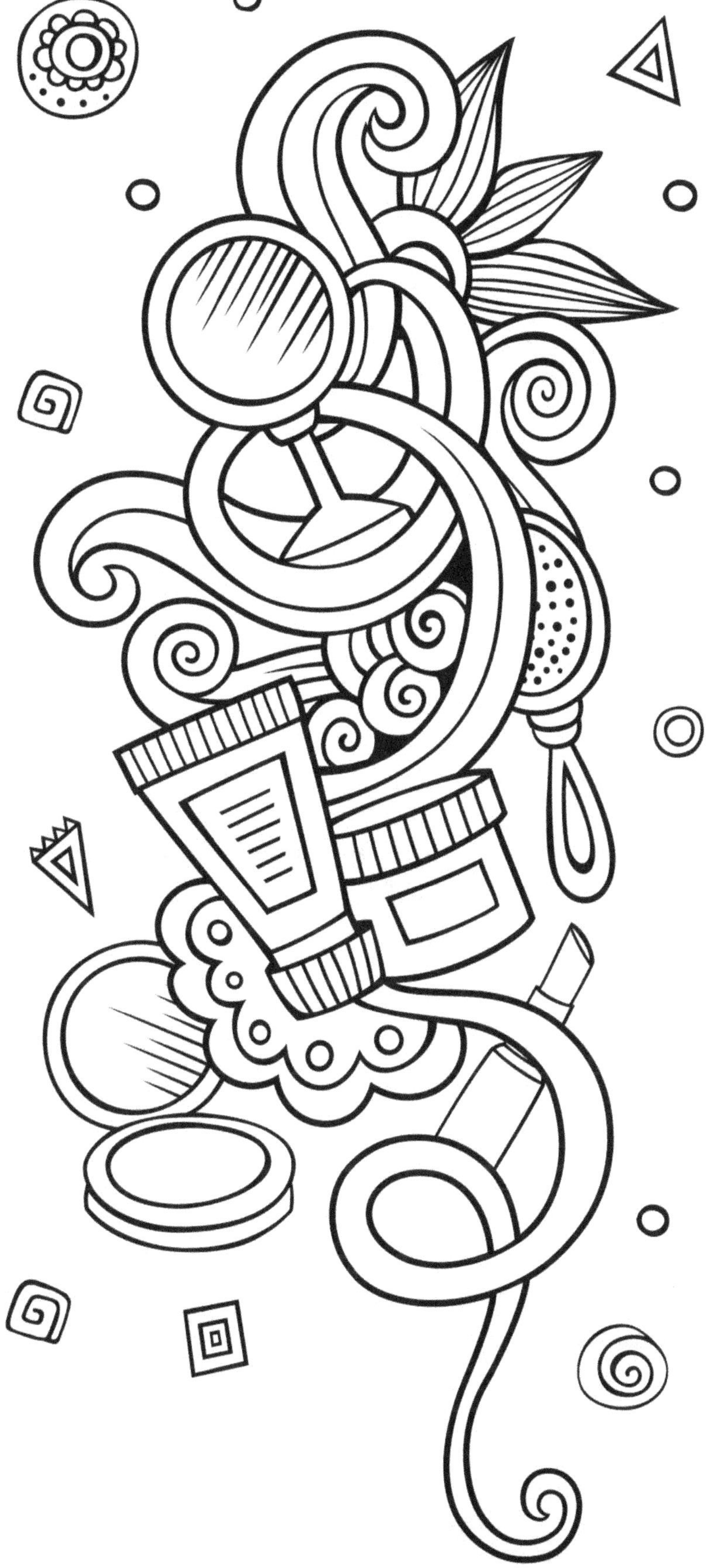

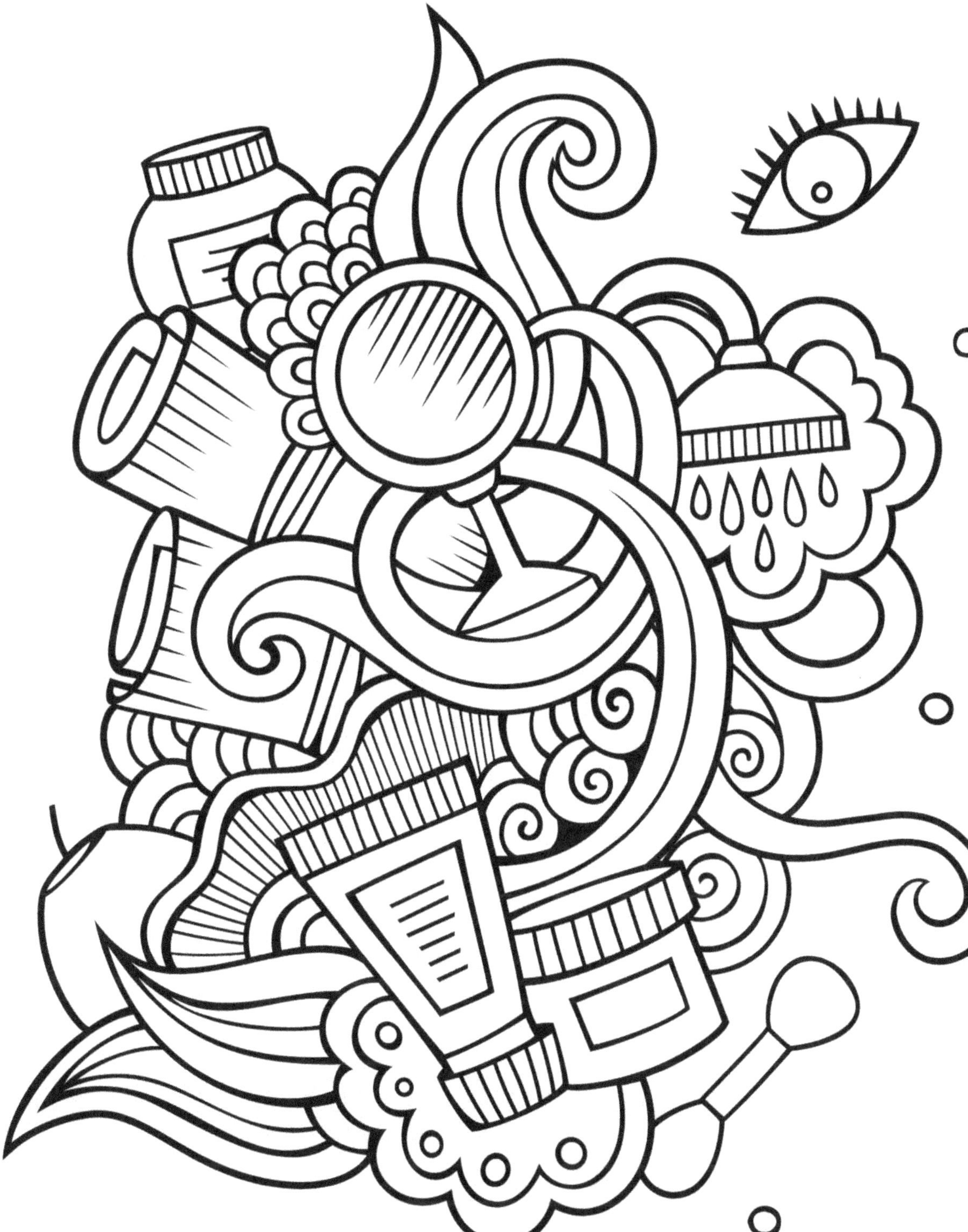

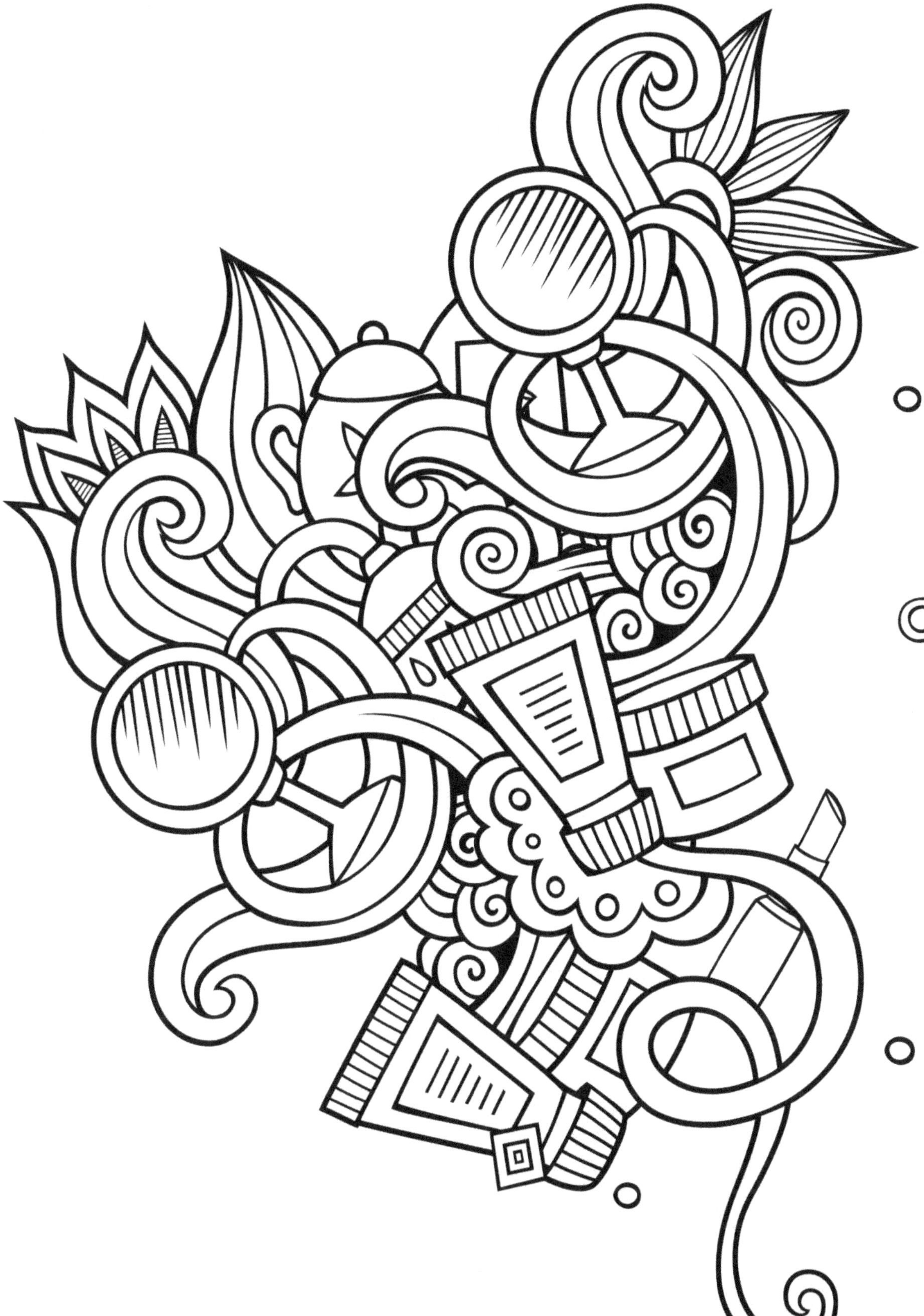

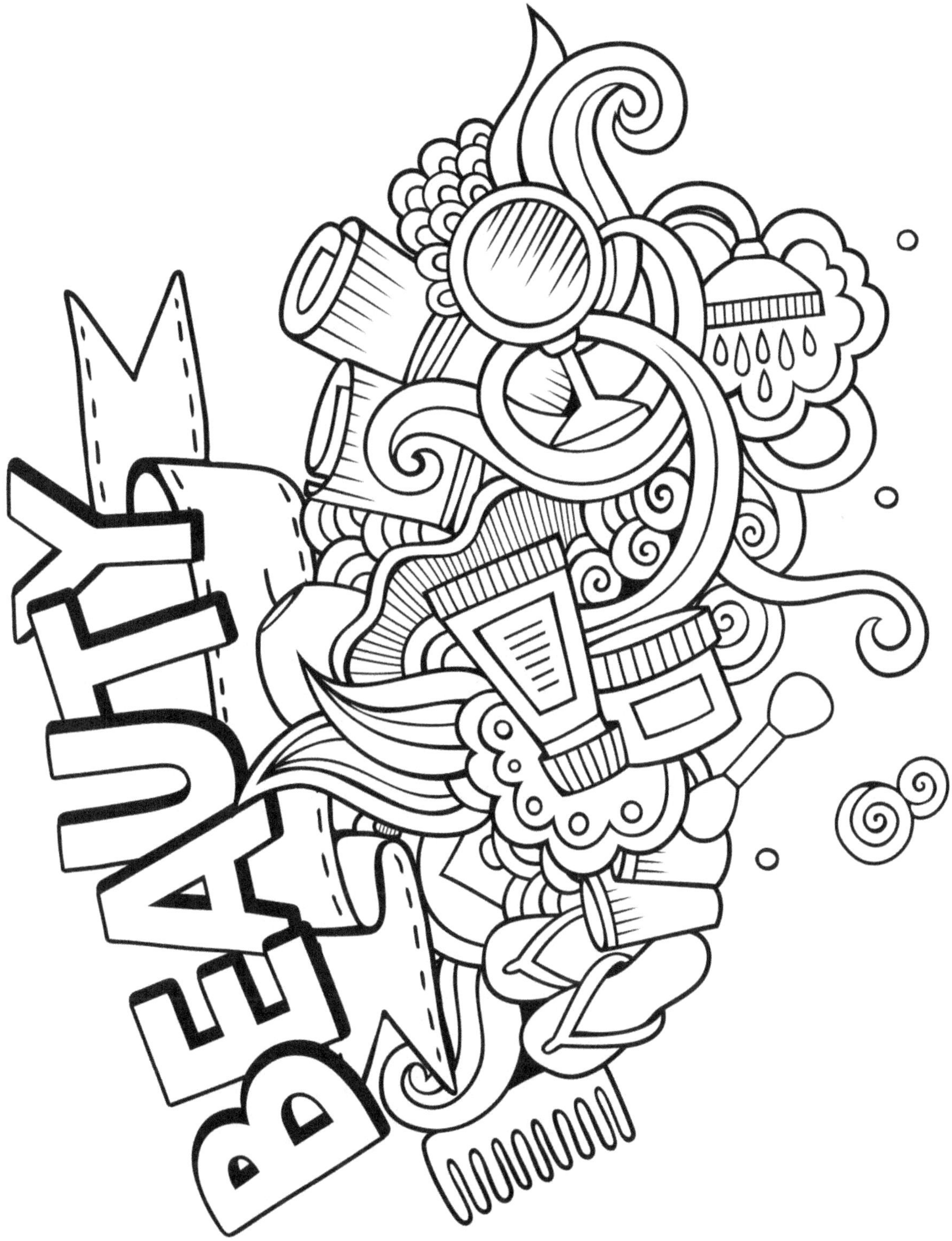
BEAUTY

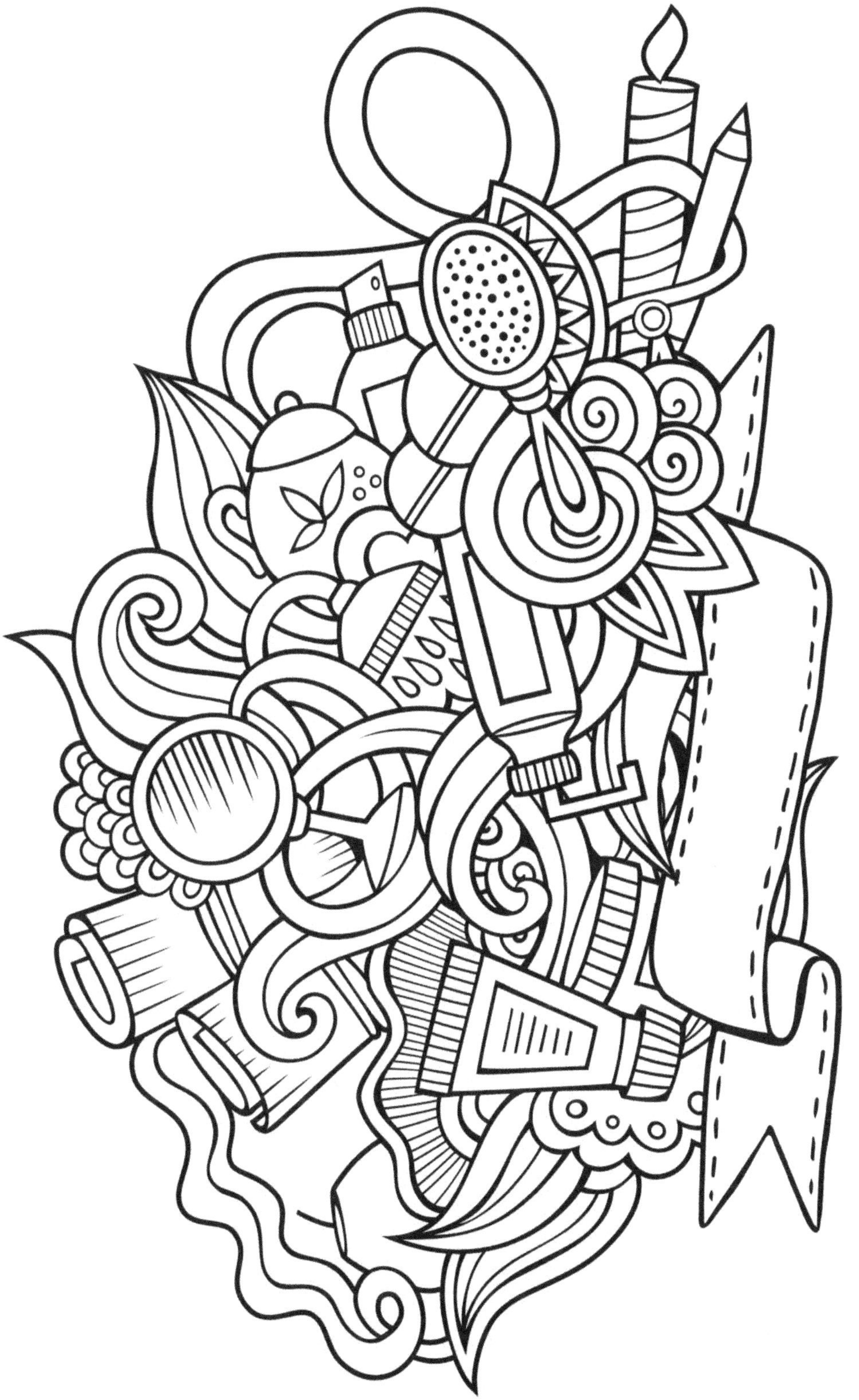

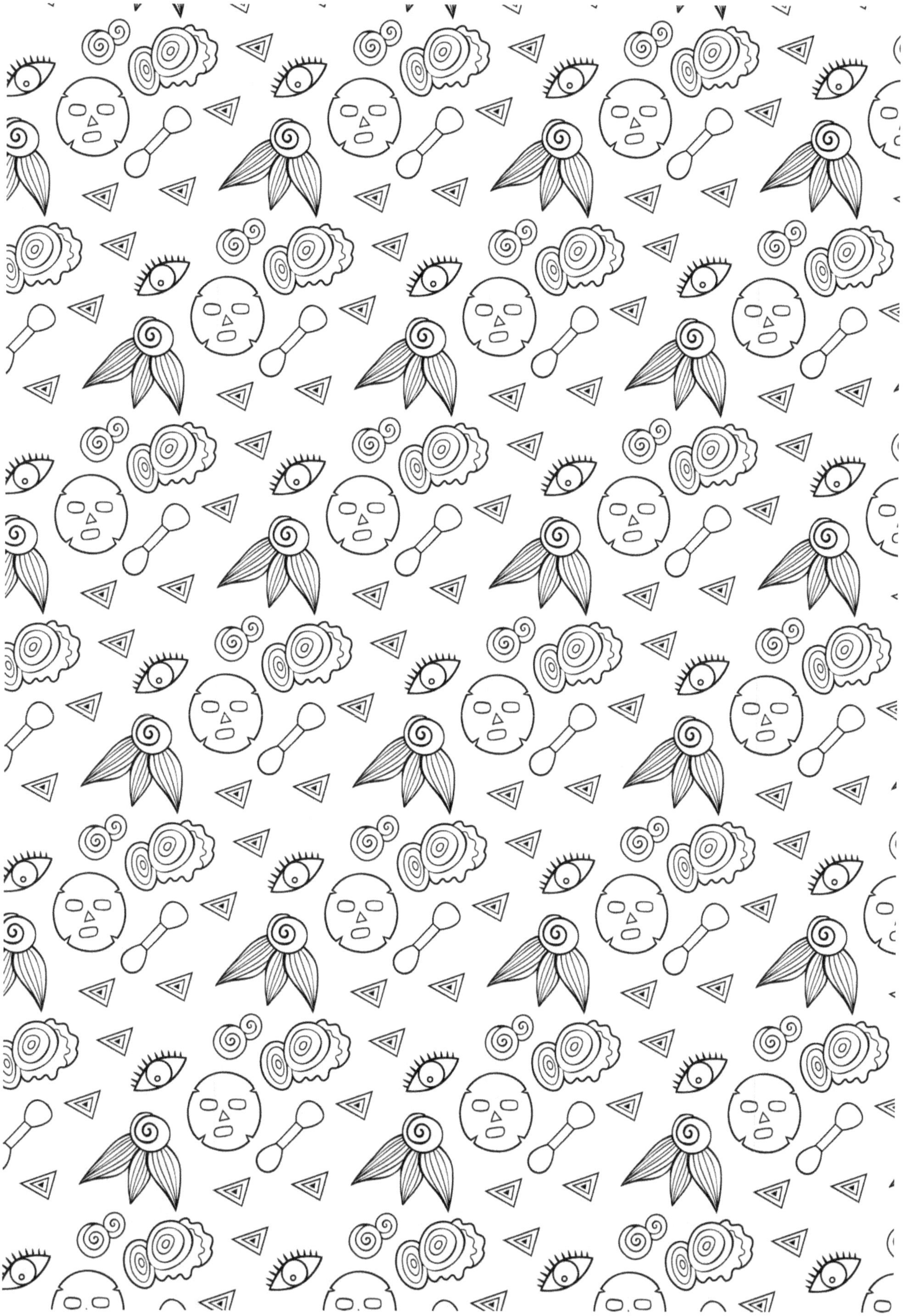

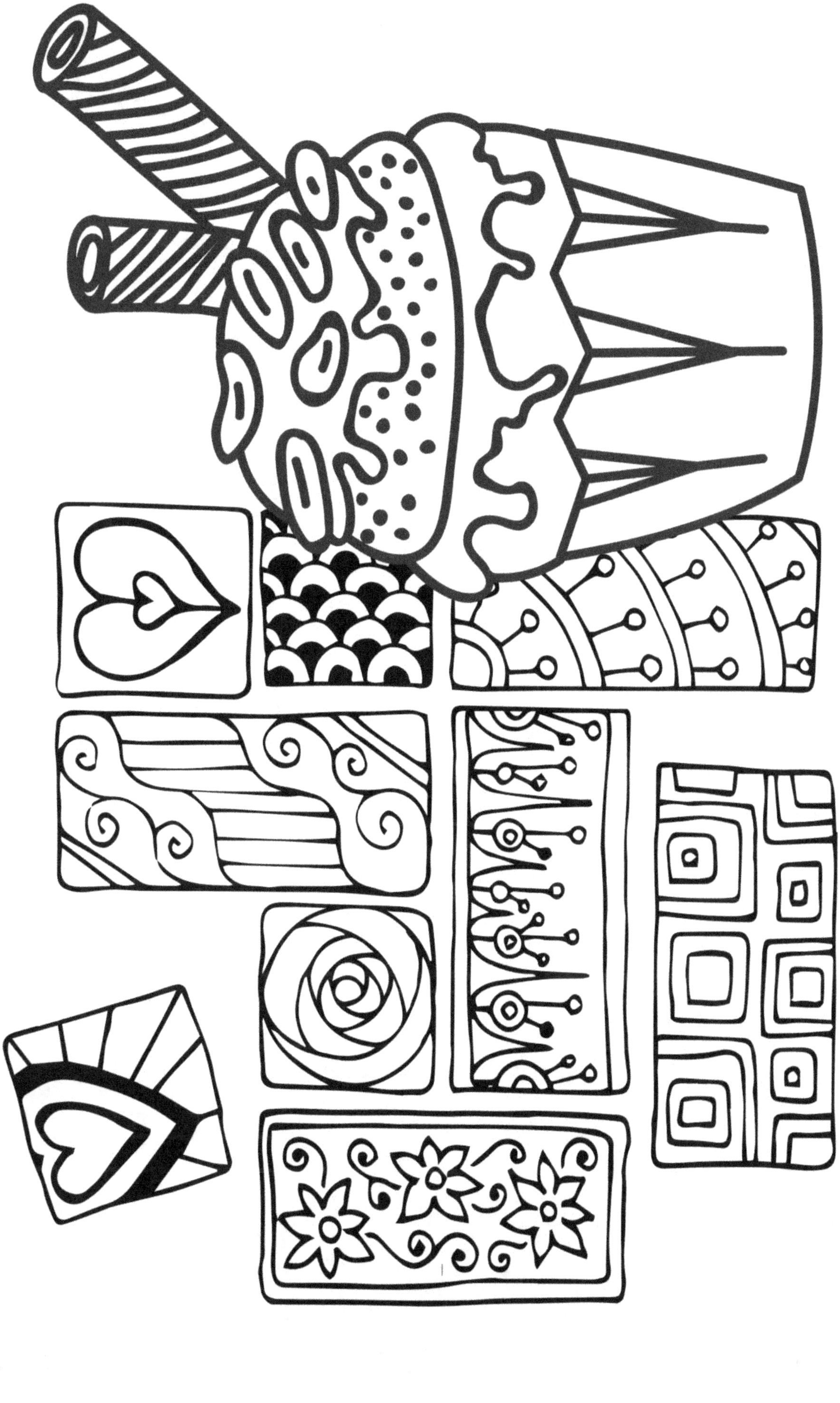

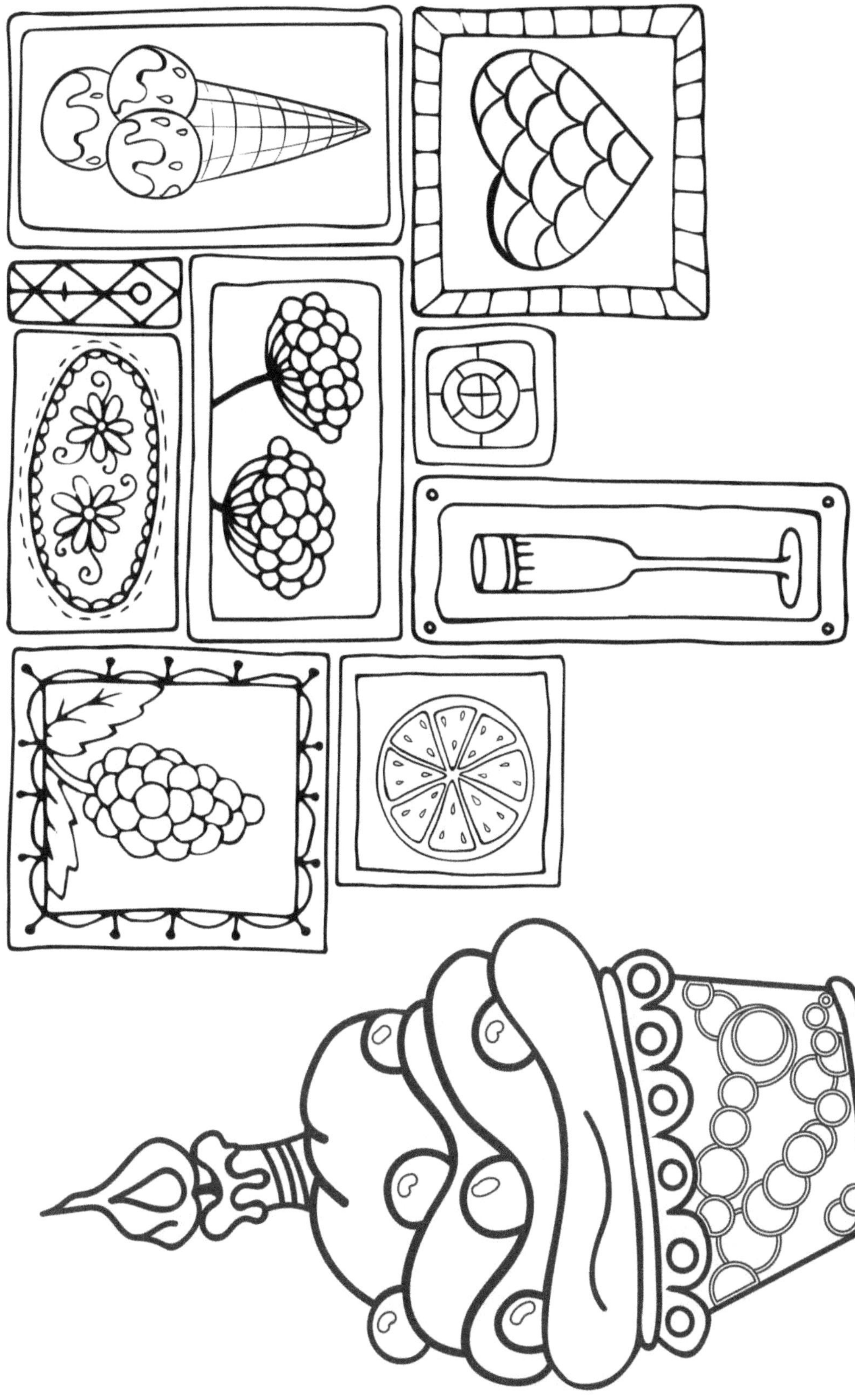

FAV

www.ingramcontent.com/pod-product-compliance
Lightning Source LLC
Chambersburg PA
CBHW081856170526
45167CB00007B/3035
* 9 7 8 1 5 4 3 0 5 0 4 5 5 *